THE FABULOUS LOST & FOUND

AND THE LITTLE JAPANESE MOUSE

WRITTEN BY MARK PALLIS
ILLUSTRATED BY PETER BAYNTON

NEU WESTEND
— PRESS —

For Kai and Tino - MP

For Hannah and Skye - PB

THE FABULOUS LOST & FOUND AND THE LITTLE JAPANESE MOUSE

First Printing, 2020
ISBN: 978-1-913595-46-3
NeuWestendPress.com

THE FABULOUS LOST & FOUND

AND THE LITTLE JAPANESE MOUSE

WRITTEN BY MARK PALLIS
ILLUSTRATED BY PETER BAYNTON

NEU WESTEND
— PRESS —

In the middle of the big city is a tiny yellow building. If anyone loses anything, this is where it ends up.

It is called the Lost and Found.

Mr and Mrs Frog keep everything safe, hoping that someday every lost watch and bag and phone and toy and shoe and cheesegrater will find its owner again.

But the shop is very small. And there are so many lost things. It is all quite a squeeze, but still, it's fabulous.

One sunny day, a little mouse walked in.

“Welcome,” said Mrs Frog. “What have you lost?”

Bōshi o nakushi chatta
“ぼうしをなくしちゃった。” said the mouse.

Mr and Mrs Frog could not speak Japanese. They had no idea what the little mouse was saying.

What shall we do? they wondered.

Maybe she's lost an umbrella. Everyone loses an umbrella at least twice, thought Mr Frog.

"Have you lost this?" asked Mr Frog.

Kasa? Chigau yo

“かさ？ちがうよ。” replied the mouse.

Then Mrs Frog remembered something
that had been handed in a few months ago...

“Is this yours?” Mrs Frog asked, holding up a chunk of cheese.

Chī zu? Chigau, kusai yo
“チーズ？ちがう、くさいよ！” said the mouse.

“Time to put that cheese in the bin dear,” said Mr Frog.

Bōshi
”Maybe the word ‘ぼうし’ means coat,” said Mr Frog.

“Now where did I put that nice yellow one?”

"Got it!" said Mr Frog.

Kō to? Chigau, bōshi o nakushi chatta

“コート？ちがう、ぼうしをなくしちゃった。”

said the mouse.

She was starting to feel a bit frustrated.

“We need to keep trying,” said Mrs Frog.

Mafurā janai yo
マフラー じゃないよ。

Pantsu janai yo
パンツ じゃないよ。

Sē tā janai yo
セーター じゃないよ。

San gurasu janai yo
サングラス じゃないよ。

Kutsu janai yo
くつ じゃないよ。

Bōshi o nakushi chatta
“ぼうしをなくしちゃった。”

said the mouse.

Jitensha nidai ja nai yo
じてんしゃ2だいじゃないよ。
Kon pyū ta janai yo
コンピューターじゃないよ。

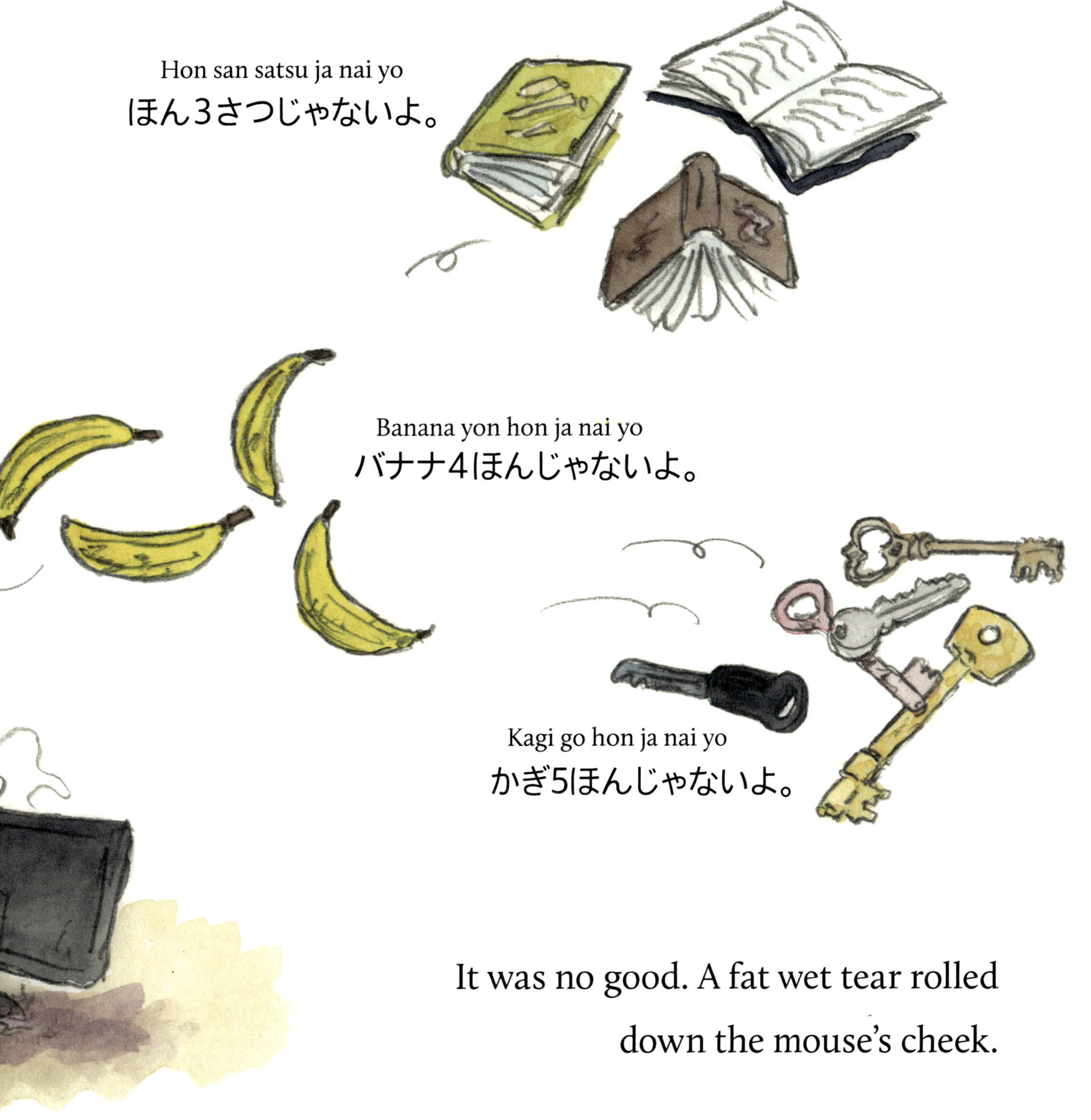

Hon san satsu ja nai yo
ほん3さつじゃないよ。

Banana yon hon ja nai yo
バナナ4ほんじゃないよ。

Kagi go hon ja nai yo
かぎ5ほんじゃないよ。

It was no good. A fat wet tear rolled down the mouse's cheek.

“How about a nice cup of tea?” asked Mrs Frog kindly.

Ochaga daisukinanda. Arigatō

“おちゃがだいすきなんだ。ありがとう。” replied the mouse. They sat together, sipping their tea and all feeling a bit sad.

Suddenly, the mouse realised she could try pointing.

She pointed at her head.

Bōshi
"ぼうし!" she said.

"I've got it!" exclaimed Mrs Frog, leaping up.

"A wig of course!" said Mrs Frog.

Katsura janai yo
"かつらじゃないよ。" said the mouse.

Aka janai yo
あかじゃないよ。

Kin patsu janai yo
きんぱつじゃないよ。

Cha patsu janai yo
ちゃぱつじゃないよ。

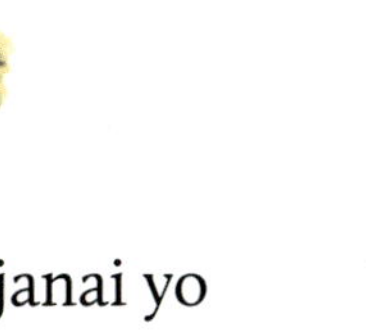

Iron'na iro no janai yo
いろんないろのじゃないよ。

Midori janai yo
みどりじゃないよ。

"What about this?" asked Mr Frog, pulling back a curtain.

Bōshi
"ぼうし!" exclaimed the mouse.

Bōshi
"Ah, so 'ぼうし' means hat. Wonderful!" cheered Mr and Mrs Frog.

"One hat left," said Mrs Frog, reaching all the way to the back of the cupboard.

"It couldn't be this old thing, could it?"

Watashi no bōshi
“わたしのぼうし。

Yatto watashi no bōshi o mitsuketa
やっとわたしのぼうしをみつけた！

Dōmo arigatō
どうもありがとう。” said the mouse.

And just like that, the mouse found her hat.

Sayōnara
"さようなら" she said, as she skipped away.
Sayōnara
"さようなら" replied Mr and Mrs Frog.

"I wonder who will come tomorrow?" said Mr Frog.

Mrs Frog put her arm around him.

"I don't know," she replied, giving him a squeeze,
"but whoever it is, we'll do our best to help."

LEARNING TO LOVE LANGUAGES

An additional language opens a child's mind, broadens their horizons and enriches their emotional life. Research has shown that the time between a child's birth and their sixth or seventh birthday is a "golden period" when they are most receptive to new languages. This is because they have an in-built ability to distinguish the sounds they hear and make sense of them. The Story-powered Language Learning Method taps into these natural abilities.

HOW THE STORY-POWERED LANGUAGE LEARNING METHOD WORKS

We create an emotionally engaging and funny story for children and adults to enjoy together, just like any other picture book. Studies show that social interaction, like enjoying a book together, is critical in language learning.

Through the story, we introduce a relatable character who speaks only in the new language. This helps build empathy and a positive attitude towards people who speak different languages. These are both important aspects in laying the foundations for lasting language acquisition in a child's life.

As the story progresses, the child naturally works with the characters to discover the meaning of a wide range of fun new words. Strategic use of humour ensures that this subconscious learning is rewarded with laughter; the child feels good and the first seeds of a lifelong love of languages are sown.

For more information and free downloads visit www.neuwestendpress.com

ALL THE BEAUTIFUL JAPANESE WORDS AND PHRASES FROM OUR STORY

ぼうしをなくしちゃった	I've lost my hat
ぼうし	hat
かさ	umbrella
チーズ	cheese
くさい	it stinks
コート	coat
マフラー	warm scarf
パンツ	trousers
サングラス	sunglasses
セーター	sweater
くつ	shoes
いち	one
に	two
さん	three
よん	four
ご	five
コンピューター	computer
ほん	book
かぎ	key
バナナ	banana
じてんしゃ	bicycle
おちゃがだいすき	I love tea
ありがとう	thank you
どうもありがとう	thanks very much
かつら	wig
あか	red
きんぱつ	blond
ちゃぱつ	brown
みどり	green
いろんないろ	multicoloured
いいえ	no
たかすぎる	too tall
おおきすぎる	too big
ちいさすぎる	too small
きつすぎる	too tight
わたしのぼうしをみつけた	I've found my hat
さようなら	goodbye

THE WORLD OF

THE FABULOUS LOST & FOUND

THIS STORY IS ALSO AVAILABLE IN...

FRENCH

SPANISH

ITALIAN

CZECH

WELSH

KOREAN

GERMAN

GREEK

SWEDISH

POLISH

SLOVAKIAN

VIETNAMESE

LATIN

PORTUGUESE

...AND MANY MORE LANGUAGES!

ENJOYED IT?
WRITE A REVIEW AND
LET US KNOW!

@MARK_PALLIS ON TWITTER
WWW.MARKPALLIS.COM

@PETERBAYNTON ON INSTAGRAM
WWW.PETERBAYNTON.COM

Made in the USA
Las Vegas, NV
07 March 2023

68693314R00024